THE OFFICIAL LEGO® ANNUAL 2013

CONTENTS

Police United

The LEGO® CITY Police have joined forces with the Forest Rangers. There is no place for crooks to hide now! Look at the pictures on the opposite page and try to find them in the scene. Then write down how many police vehicles you can see.

4439

POLICE

A

B

C

D

POLICE VEHICLES

Quick Snack

Prison Break

A crook is digging a tunnel under the police station to help his friends escape. He can't find the way to their cell, but he can hear people talking. Match the pairs of speech bubbles to the pictures, so that he knows where to dig.

A

FOREST RANGER! BRING THE RECOVERED MONEY BACK TO THE BANK AS SOON AS POSSIBLE!

GEE, THOSE CITY FOLKS ARE ALWAYS IN A RUSH . . .

B

WHY DO I ALWAYS HAVE TO DO THINGS MYSELF? PRISON BREAK, TOO?

ZZZZZ . . .

C

MMM! THIS IS THE BEST HOT CHOCOLATE I'VE EVER HAD!

CAN I HAVE SOME, TOO, PLEASE?

D

LOOKS LIKE WE'RE GONNA HAVE A GUEST . . .

THE BEAR AGAIN?! SHOULD I CALL FOR BACK UP?

Latecomer

ANOTHER MORNING IN LEGO CITY.

HENRY WAKES UP . . .

OH NO! I OVERSLEPT!

. . . ONE HOUR TOO LATE.

TAXI!

STEP ON IT! I CAN'T BE LATE!

FIVE MINUTES LATER, BY THE LAUNCH PLATFORM . . .

FINALLY!

STOP 02

TAXI

JM 7937

Bicycle Trouble

The ambulance crew are helping a cyclist who has had an accident. Do you know what device is used for hearing a patient's heartbeat? Work out its name by reading the letters opposite the peaks of the chart and writing them in the space below.

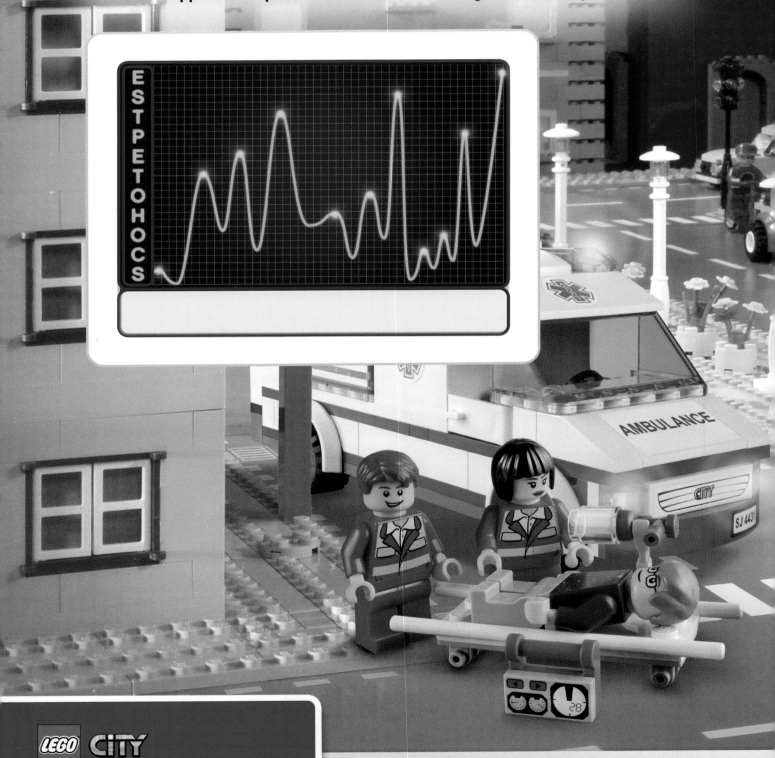

Find the cyclist's lost helmet and all the parts of his bicycle in amongst the pile of rubbish, before the refuse collectors take it all away in their lorry.

CITY

HA 4432

Forest Fire Brigade

The brave Forest Fire Brigade is always ready for action! Take a look at the picture and try to remember it - you will be asked about it later! Then match the silhouettes to the correct firefighters.

The Greatest Fan

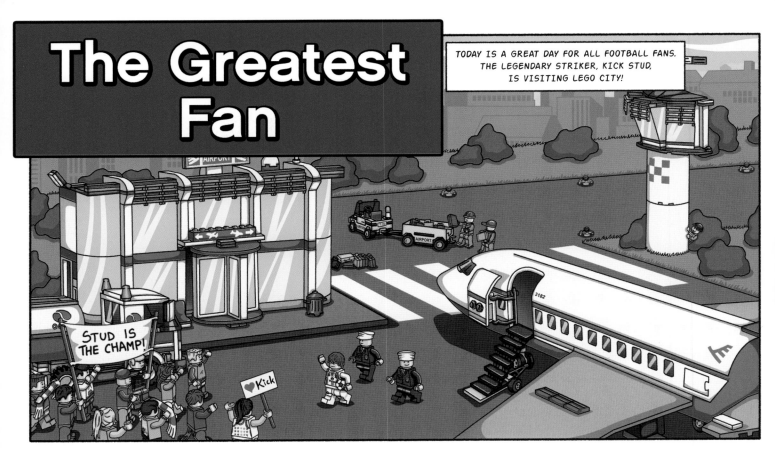

WATCHING ALL THOSE WESTERNS TURNED OUT TO BE A GOOD IDEA AFTER ALL!

UHH!

WELL, WELL. IF IT ISN'T LIGHT-FINGERED LARRY. YOU'RE A WANTED MAN!

HAVE YOU SWITCHED TO STEALING NOTEBOOKS?

YOU DON'T UNDERSTAND!

I'VE ALWAYS WANTED TO GET STUD'S AUTOGRAPH! I'M HIS BIGGEST FAN!!

SO WHY HAVEN'T YOU SIMPLY ASKED HIM FOR ONE?

BECAUSE . . . BECAUSE I'M TOO SHY.

IT'S VERY KIND OF KICK TO AGREE TO SIGN SUCH A STRANGE OBJECT.

THE THINGS SOME STARS WILL DO FOR THEIR FANS!

KICK STUD

True or False?

How much can you remember from the picture on pages 16-17?
Without looking back, mark the statements below with a "T"
for "true" or an "F" for "false".

1 ☐ There were nine firefighters in the picture.

2 ☐ The firefighters had put out all the flames.

3 ☐ One firefighter was holding a chain saw.

4 ☐ There was a girl with a blue cup in the picture.

5 ☐ There was a bear hiding in the trees.

6 ☐ There was one aeroplane in the picture.

HQ to Pilot!

Part of a message from the Fire Brigade's headquarters has become scrambled.
Cross out every letter that appears twice on the screen to help the pilot work out what to do next.

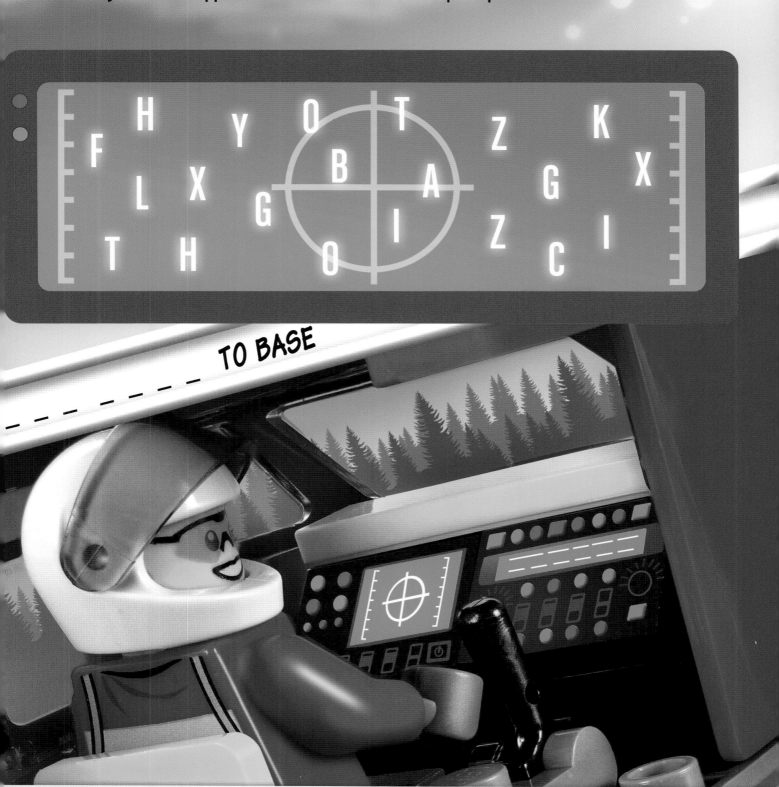

TO BASE

Lucky Day

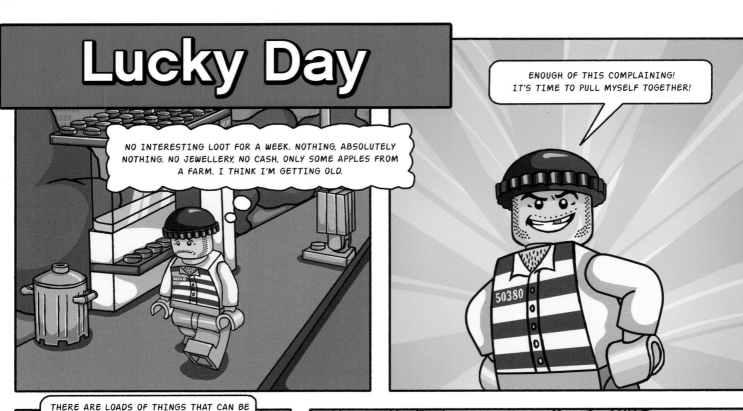

Just One Wish

Little Red Riding Hood wishes she could be someone else for a change. Luckily for her, a helpful genie has offered to make her wish come true. Can you work out which of the characters opposite she would like to be?

WHAT IS YOUR WISH?

I WISH:
- I NEVER HAD TO WEAR RED CLOTHES AGAIN
- I NEVER HAD TO WEAR DRESSES
- I NEVER HAD TO WEAR A HEAD-DRESS
- I WAS A COOL GIRL
- I PERFORMED ON STAGE

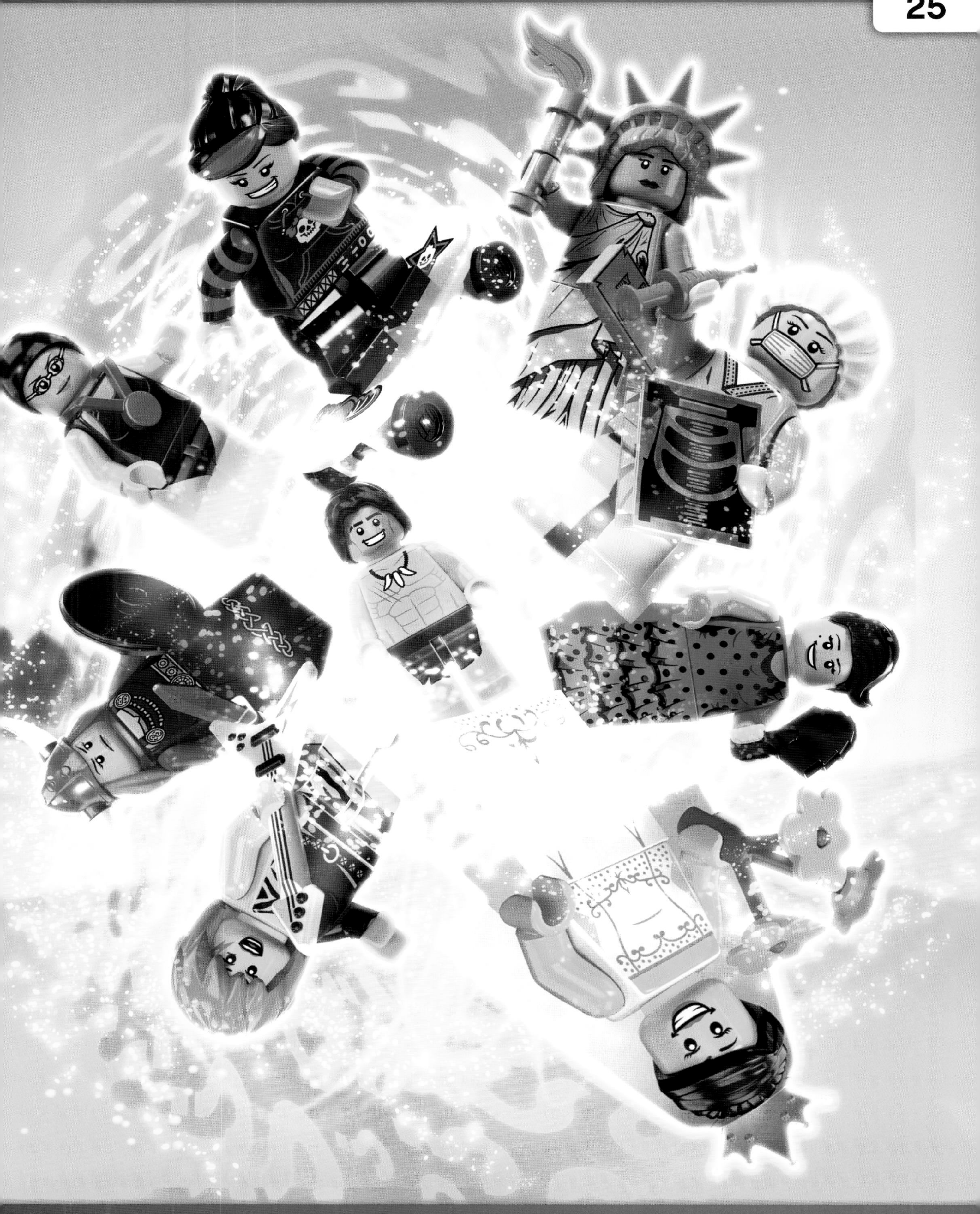

Missing One

Can you spot which person is missing in rows 1–3?
Write the correct letter into the empty space in each sequence.

To :) or not to :)?

Walter has made a note of his five favourite 'smiley face' emoticons and stuck it to his monitor. How quickly can you find them on his screen?

:) :D ;)
:P :(

:> :* ;< :# :+ ;? :C ;D

;P :: :& :) :< ;* :O ;[

:] :P :/ ;> :} :| ;{ :F

B) :X :Q :_(:@ ;^ ;[;)

:D :\ B[:T :(__

C:\

Wrong Stage

NOBODY ELSE HAS EVER LANDED ON THIS PLANET.

THERE COULD BE MANY SURPRISES FOR US HERE.

AGHHHHEYEYAYAYAAAAAAR!!!

TARZAN IS ALWAYS MAKING A NUISANCE OF HIMSELF.

BANDIT?!

HOWDY!

STOP THE CAMERA!!!

WHAT'S GOING ON HERE?

THEY'RE SHOOTING A WESTERN ON THE NEXT STAGE, AND A TARZAN MOVIE BEHIND THIS WALL.

DON'T COMPLAIN. YESTERDAY, THEY WERE FILMING A SEA BATTLE SCENE UPSTAIRS . . .

. . . THE WATER LEAKED THROUGH THE CEILING AND FLOODED OUR APACHES' WIGWAMS.

AND ABOVE US THEY'RE STARTING A MOVIE ABOUT A GIANT KANGAROO JUMPING ON A CITY!

OH, NO! IT'S DRIVING ME CRAZY!

Broken Photo

A robot has accidentally knocked over a souvenir photo from a space mission and broken it. Can you find the missing pieces? Be careful . . . not all the pieces will fit!

Ready for Discharge

This patient had a broken rib, but thankfully it is better now. Before she lets him go home, the surgeon needs his current x-ray photo. Help her find the correct photo on the light board.

Arrive on Time

Hamish the Highlander is running late for a bagpipe lesson and it makes him very angry! Help him reach his teacher by guiding him across the grid using the key below.

Right   **Left**   **Up**   **Down**

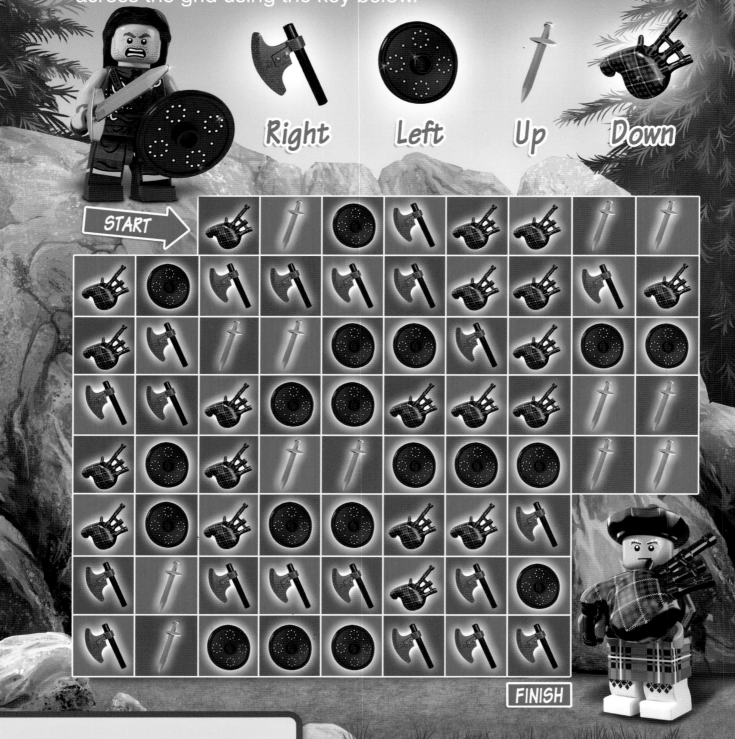

START

FINISH

Golden Treasure

Who has more gold: Neptune or the Leprechaun? The number on each bar is found by adding the numbers on the two bars below. Work out the numbers on the top bars to find the winner.

NINJA RIDES

There is a new menace to Ninjago! But the Masters of Spinjitzu have amazing vehicles with powerful weapons to stop the enemy. Match the descriptions to the names of the vehicles, then add in the names of their ninja pilots.

With activated ice-sprayer this vehicle can skid out of trouble on any terrain! It belongs to . . .

Massive and solid as a rock this vehicle is armed with a rock shooter and ninja blades. It belongs to . . .

This super-fast jet strikes like a flashing lightning from the sky to defeat any enemy! It belongs to . . .

It has power, speed, two wheels and razor sharp blades . . . and a sharp rider, too! It belongs to . . .

1.

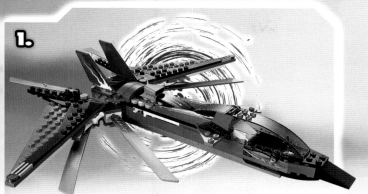

STORM FIGHTER

2.

TREAD ASSAULT

3.

BLADE CYCLE

4.

SNOW MOBILE

JAY   **ZANE**   **KAI**   **COLE**

Fiery Task

WHAT'S WRONG?

Four terrifying snake tribes have united to destroy Ninjago! But they won't defeat Sensei Wu's team without a fight. There is something wrong with this scene, though. Can you spot the 6 odd things in the picture?

THE PICTURE TO THE STORY

One of the brave ninja has a dangerous mission to accomplish. Read the story below and look carefully at the three pictures. Which one illustrates the story? Write the correct number in the empty box.

The ninja silently sneaked into the shrine. His mission was to retrieve the anti-venom hidden inside the golden Venomari staff. As he tiptoed around the toxic snake slime to reach the staff, he saw two small snakes guarding the temple. It was too late to back away – the snakes had seen him too! Suddenly, one of them lunged at the intruder. But the white-garbed ninja drew his sword fast! The green snake never got close enough to stop him . . .

1.

2.

3.

NINJA MIND PRACTICE

The snake warriors are cunning and sneaky enemies. In order to defeat them, the ninja practise Spinjitzu as well as mind skills. Can you work out what numbers should replace the symbols below to make the correct equations?

WORDSEARCH

Find the names of eleven Ninjago heroes and villains in the grid below. The words may be written across, down or diagonally. One of the names belongs to someone who is following in his father's footsteps to become a supervillain. Can you point to his name?

```
A R I N A F G H N F E T W A
P S H Y P N O B R A I J U L
U I O A U L R U G N E R U L
I V K E H O I Z E G B S G O
K L E I J P L A R P Q E T Y
L T B N O T L N W Y A N H D
C U F H O T A E A R R S R G
O R B M R M S T Z E N E Y A
L W N E T I A O Y A M I U R
E B I R K R R R Y V K W I M
R Y U O Y A I M I X P U H A
W J A Y A M I I A R O R N D
E M M L I O M T W Q L J R O
U C O N S T R I C T A I Q N
```

HYPNOBRAI, FANGPYRE, CONSTRICTAI, VENOMARI, SENSEI WU, LLOYD GARMADON, KAI, COLE, ZANE, JAY, NYA

PICTURE PUZZLE

The snakes are full of nasty surprises! With their venomous bite, the Fangpyre can turn anything – even machines – into one of their own! Put the mixed pieces of the picture in the correct order to see an awesome battle scene.

THE FOUR ELEMENTS

The following sequence of the ninja elemental symbols appears only once in the grid below. Use your keen ninja eyes to spot it!

THE BREAKOUT

Red alert! A group of villains has escaped from Hero Factory's Storage Facility! Find out more about the villains below. You can only read their names by using a mirror.

BLACK PHANTOM

The mastermind of this unprecedented breakout. Smart and powerful, he stands head and shoulders above friends and foes alike. His razor sabre staff is swift to deal out injustice, and his Arachnix drone can instantly clone itself to make life miserable for enemies!

TOXIC REAPA

This native of the jungle planet Z'chaya has got powerful crushing claws, laser cutters, and a tank of toxic waste that melts and contaminates anything it touches. If he's not caught in time, he may infect the larvae on his home planet, creating an entire army of evil insects!

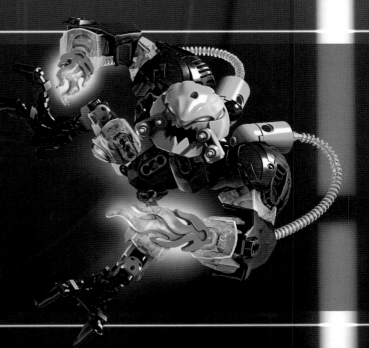

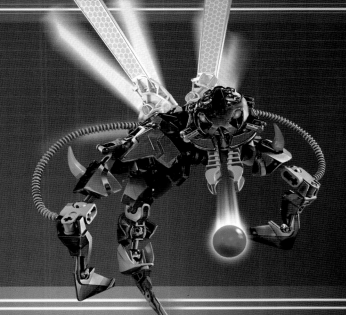

THORNRAXX

He loves to fly and buzz at enemies, jabbing at them with his stinger or venom spitter. He is the meanest of all the notoriously short-tempered inhabitants of his hive planet. The witnesses of his dreadful exploits agree they'll be watching the skies for the rest of their lives.

JAWBLADE

Swift as a shark, with crushing jaws, razor fins and magma blades, this villain is far more at home underwater than on land. He's heading for the water planet Scylla to obtain Oxidium, a fast-acting rusting agent. He'd use it to instantly rust any hero who comes to cuff him.

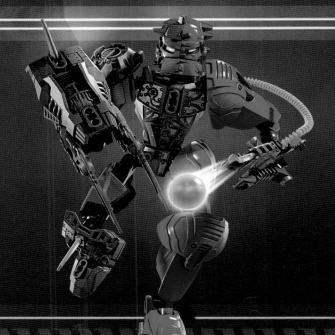

SPLITFACE

He is part organic, part mechanical, but all evil. His organic self prefers to use his nasty infecticide, while his mechanical self relies on the vicious shredding claw. Both weapons are dangerous, especially when he can't agree with himself and uses them at the same time.

WARRIOR DOMINOES

Look carefully at the domino chain. Which of the spare dominoes will complete it?
Write the correct letters in the blank spaces, but be careful: one piece doesn't fit in the chain.

SPOT THE DIFFERENCE

The heroes are eager to bring the villains back to the Hero Factory's Storage Facility, but they are not fully equipped for the mission . . . Can you spot the 10 missing elements in the picture below?

CATCH THE VILLAINS

Mission: bring the fugitives back to Hero Factory! If left uncaptured, they could do incredible damage. Lead Rocka through the maze and catch all the villains on your way to Black Phantom. Just don't forget to handcuff him, too!

Page 4
Police United

Page 8
Prison Break

Page 12-13
Bicycle Trouble
STETHOSCOPE

Page 16
Forest Fire Brigade

Page 20
True or False?
1 – T, 2 – F, 3 – T, 4 – F, 5 – T, 6 – F

Page 21
HQ to Pilot!
Fly back to base.

Page 24
Just One Wish

Page 26
Missing One

Page 27
To :) or not to :) ?

```
:> :* ;< :# :+ ;? :C ;D
;P :: :& :) :< ;* :O ;[
:] :P :/ ;> :) :I ;{ :F
B) :X :Q :_( :@ ;^ ;[ ;)
:D :\ B[ :T :( __
```

answers

Page 30
Broken Photo

Page 31
Ready for Discharge

Page 32
Arrive on Time

Page 33
Golden Treasure

Page 34
NINJA RIDES

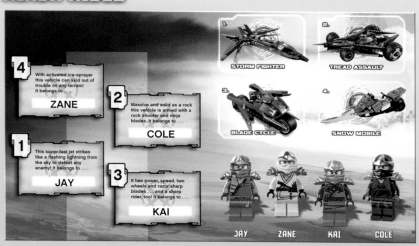

4 With activated ice-sprayer this vehicle can skid out of trouble on any terrain! It belongs to . . .
ZANE

2 Massive and solid as a rock this vehicle is armed with a rock shooter and ninja blades. It belongs to . . .
COLE

1 This super-fast jet strikes like a flashing lightning from the sky to defeat any enemy! It belongs to . . .
JAY

3 It has power, speed, two wheels and razor sharp blades . . . and a sharp rider, too! It belongs to . . .
KAI

1. STORM FIGHTER
2. TREAD ASSAULT
3. BLADE CYCLE
4. SNOW MOBILE

JAY   ZANE   KAI   COLE

Page 38
WHAT'S WRONG?

Page 40
THE PICTURE TO THE STORY

Page 42

NINJA MIND PRACTICE

2 3 1 5

Page 43

WORDSEARCH

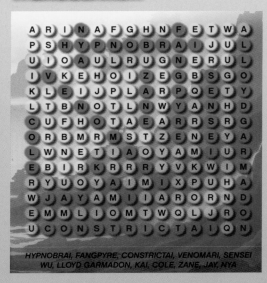

HYPNOBRAI, FANGPYRE, CONSTRICTAI, VENOMARI, SENSEI WU, LLOYD GARMADON, KAI, COLE, ZANE, JAY, NYA

Lloyd Garmadon is following in his father's footsteps to become a supervillain.

Page 46

PICTURE PUZZLE

1 2 3 4 5 6

Page 47

THE FOUR ELEMENTS

Page 48

THE BREAKOUT

**Black Phantom
Toxic Reapa
Thornraxx
Jawblade
Splitface**

Page 50

WARRIOR DOMINOES

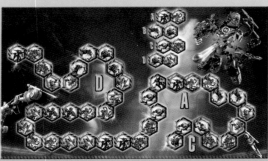

Piece B doesn't fit in the chain.

Page 52

SPOT THE DIFFERENCE

Page 54

CATCH THE VILLAINS

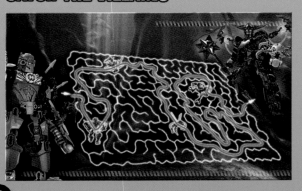

answers

FREE!

LEGO Club Jr. (0-6)

LEGO Club Magazine (7+)

LEGO Club Magazine

www.LEGOclub.com

LEGO Club Email News

BECOME A LEGO® CLUB MEMBER
AND GET FREE LEGO CLUB MAGAZINES!

Your FREE membership includes:

- 5 Magazines a year! · Exclusive building steps!
- Cool Creations! · Sneak previews of new sets!
- Competitions, comics, puzzles and activities!

Plus email newsletters and our awesome website!

SIGN UP TODAY AT
www.LEGOclub.com

LEGO club ™

LEGO Ninjago Jay
▼ With Minifigure

LEGO Star Wars Darth Vader
Giant Minifigure Alarm Clock ▼

LEGO Star Wars™ Darth Maul
▼ With Minifigure

LEGO Creator
▼ With Building Toy

www.legowatches.com
LEGO® Watches and Clocks

ClicTime